Dedicated to Professor David Josephson, Brown University

Thank for your interest in Academic Life Coaching and this workbook.

Although this workbook offers a complete program, it's really designed to be used - and you will get the most benefit - working with a trained Academic Life Coach.

To see a list of coaches certified to use this material, please visit
www.academiclifecoaching.com

Table of Contents

Introduction **6**

    Our Story, Your Benefit 6

    The Academic Life Coaching Program............................8

    The Four Cornerstones of Academic Life Coaching 9

    The Four Myths of Working with a Coach 12

    Guidelines for the Academic Life Coaching Program.................14

Academic Life Coaching Curriculum **19**

Session One (Academic Success, Part 1)

    Wheel of Life...23

    Well-Formed Outcomes 26

    Learning Styles: Visual, Audio, Kinesthetic 32

    Design the Client-Coach-Parent Alliance 37

Session Two (Academic Success, Part 2)

    Thinking Styles 43

    Core Motivation 49

    Motivation Styles 57

    Conditional vs. Intrinsic Motivation 58

Motivation Away from Bad Stuff vs. Toward Good Stuff 61

Motivation for the Sake of Self vs. Other 64

Session Three (Academic Success, Part 3)

Vision, Creating a Tape/Structure to Make it Real 69

Recipe for Academic Success 71

Systems and Organization 73

Dropping Anchors...78

Session Four (Personal Fluency Part 1)

Assumption Chart 83

Busting Limiting Beliefs 87

Signature Perspectives 89

Core Motivation Check-Up 90

Session Five (Personal Fluency Part 2)

Trademarked Values...95

Making Decisions 97

Future-Pacing..98

Self-Alignment: Getting Over Jet-Lag.......................................99

Session Six (Personal Fluency, Part 3)

Inner-Critic 103

Future-Self 105

Session Seven (Personal Leadership, Part 1)

Powerful Relationships 111

Building Empathy 113

Session Eight (Personal Leadership, Part 2)

Identifying Your Passions 119

Leadership Styles with Core Motivation (review of growth and progress)120

Session Nine (Personal Leadership, Part 3)

Leadership Projects 125

Mission Statements 129

Session Ten (Personal Leadership, Part 4)

Resilience 133

Celebration 134

Designing the Future 135

Completion 138

Introduction

Our Story, Your Benefit

You hold in your hands a simple, yet powerful program that has helped thousands of students succeed academically, athletically, and personally. Yet the program is an accident. It almost never came to be. I just happened to be in the right place at the right time with the right idea. And I was lucky enough to know it.

I graduated from Brown University in 2003 with a degree in Classics and went directly into teaching high school Latin. Soon after going into teaching I heard about Life Coaching, and at first I was skeptical. I mean, the name, "Life Coaching" is a little cheesy, and it's hard to describe what exactly a Life Coach does. But as I learned more about Life Coaching, I realized the concepts were not only useful but essential to living a fulfilled and effective life.

I remember sitting in my first course wondering, "Why did it take so long for me to learn this?" and "What if I had these skills in high school?" That thought became the genesis of the Academic Life Coaching program.

When I returned to teaching that fall, I realized that I had classroom after classroom of eager students willing to try out the concepts in their own lives. Essentially I had a laboratory at my fingertips with dozens of students each year helping me create and refine a body of exercises and concepts that really work.

Now <u>YOU</u> get the benefit of those hundreds of students who helped create and refine this program.

When you complete this program you will:

- Apply your learning style to earn better grades more easily
- Understand your motivation style and become more proactive
- Reduce stress because you know how to create effective systems
- Become more confident and excited about your future
- Write more successful college applications because you'll naturally demonstrate the skills admission officers are looking for

The program has evolved to a team of life coaches who are trained to deliver this program and help their clients attain a high degree of success. If you're reading this book, you're probably fortunate enough to work with one of these coaches. If you want to find a coach who's been trained to deliver this curriculum, you can find the profiles of coaches at www.academiclifecoaching.com.

The Academic Life Coaching Program

Academic Life Coaching (ALC) is about exercising leadership in your life as well as in school, at home, and in your community. It's as simple as identifying what you really want and as complex as navigating challenging relationships. It applies concepts of positive psychology and sports psychology to your life. In short, it's a powerful tool to help ensure that you are living the life you most want to live.

The ALC program works. It works because the concepts are solid, and the coaches who are trained to deliver the program really know their stuff. I highly recommend that if you go through this program, you use a Certified Life Coach, especially a coach from a company like Top Ten Skills that specifically works with Middle and High School students. Having the help of a trained professional makes a big difference, and it's worth the investment many times over.

The ALC program delivers twenty-four concepts over ten sessions. Each session is designed to last forty-five to fifty minutes and to be completed with a Certified Life Coach. You can do this program solo, and you'll gain a lot of benefit from using these concepts. But much of the dramatic success of the program happens from the magic of working with a trained coach.

The timing of the program is important. I don't recommend going through all the sessions in a weekend or rushing the program. The ALC program delivers twenty four concepts over ten sessions, and I've found it best to spread the sessions out to once a week or once every two weeks. It's important to take time between sessions to put the concepts into action and really try them out in your life. You want the program to have a long-term impact, and stretching out the learning over a few months is a great way to ensure you're really changing your habits, not just learning interesting and useful concepts.

The Four Cornerstones of Academic Life Coaching

The ALC program has four cornerstones that comprise the program. These cornerstones provide a foundation for students to thrive, not just academically in school but throughout their life. If something is not working as well as it could, one of these four cornerstones is missing. The ACL program helps students put all four in place.

First Cornerstone: Academic Systems

The first three sessions of the ALC program focus on providing a foundation for creating a sustainable system for you to consistently get the grades you want without stressing out. To begin, you'll determine your learning and academic thinking style as well as your motivation and personality type. You'll also learn tools and exercises to put what you learn into practice. To finish the cornerstone, you'll learn how to create systems that make your life easier and how to identify the little things to do differently that make a big difference.

Second Cornerstone: Personal Fluency

The second third of the program focuses on increasing your self-awareness and building your fluency with your thoughts, emotions, and habits. We each have our internal language made up of our internal dialogue, empowering and limiting beliefs, assumptions and perspectives just to name a few of the parts of speech that the fourth, fifth, and sixth sessions address. When you learn how to speak your language, you will soon discover what action you need to take to be more fulfilled and effective and your stress level will go way down. This third of the program is a constant train of "Aha" moments that build the second cornerstone of interpersonal skills and foundation of personal fluency.

Third Cornerstone: Leadership and College

The third cornerstone is personal leadership that naturally leads to your creating an outstanding college application. Leadership is not necessarily having a "leadership position" such as being the president of a club or captain on a sports team. Leadership is more about having a vision of what's possible, what you want to create, and the impact you want to have on your community. College admission officers are looking for positive examples of leadership. They want leaders, people who have the vision and the ability to create experiences for others to take part in and share, at their campus. From the point-of-view of leadership, you look at yourself and your action differently. You also add more meaning and fulfillment to your life. Leadership is one of the most important skills you can develop. The third cornerstone of the ALC program is designed to help you understand your particular brand of leadership.

Fourth Cornerstone: Support Team

The final cornerstone is present throughout the program, and at times, especially the first, fourth, and final session, you will address the issue of consciously designing your support team. Asking for help can be a challenge. For many it represents the admission that you can't figure it out on your own or that you aren't enough. School teaches us that asking for help when it counts, such as on a test or quiz, is cheating. Of course cheating is wrong, but outside of school, asking for help, especially when it counts the most, is a characteristic of strength. Learning when and how to ask for help effectively is an important skill that leads to your creating a network and community of people who are committed to supporting you and providing help when you need it. In time, you will also give back and help others; and really, the giving and receiving of help is a cornerstone of fully participating in your community.

The program is designed to complete after the ten sessions. It's a complete program, and yet, like life, we circle around to deal with issues and challenges that we've dealt with before. The purpose of this workbook is twofold. The first is that it's a structure and a guide for you to work with your coach, learn the concepts, and integrate the ideas in your life. The second, a reminder for you to refer back to and continue to use the tools in your life. It's both a guide and a reminder. In my own life, I cycle through the sessions, and each time I do, I add the understanding of all the concepts and sessions I've recently completed to my life.

On the one hand, the program is linear: you learn the concepts, apply them to your life, and you get great value for your effort and time. On the other hand, the program is cyclical. You have the opportunity to circle back through each concept and session with an ever deepening understanding of your personal fluency as well as tools and concepts that work really well for you. You begin to combine different tools and become creative in solving the challenges you meet in your life. It's a beautiful process and at its core the nexus of your life has changed. No longer are you a passive participant reacting to the demands placed on you by others, but rather you become a proactive creator of what you want to do with your life. Once you make that subtle but fundamental shift, your life takes off to a level that goes well beyond your dreams.

The Four Myths of Working with a Coach

When I first heard about Life Coaching, I was skeptical. Could it really deliver value? How does it work? What exactly does a coach do? And these were just a few of the questions in my mind. I also realized that I had a few assumptions about coaching that turned out to be untrue.

The following are the top four myths about life coaching and the Academic Life Coaching Program.

Myth #1: Working with a coach means something is wrong with me.

Reality: The top performers from professional athletes to business executives all work with coaches. If you really want to perform at the top of your game, you need to have an outside perspective to help get you there, and coaching - whether it's sports, executive, or life coaching - is designed to help people get where they want to go. In fact the name *coach* comes from the British use of the word meaning *bus*. Literally, a coach helps you get where you want to go.

Coaching is not counseling. It's not about sharing your deepest fears or emotions while trying to diagnose a problem. Coaching is focused on helping you have more positive, sustainable action in your life.

Academic Life Coaching is focused on giving you the concepts that help will help you navigate high school and college (as well as your college application).

Myth #2: This program is going to be a lot more work, and I already have too much to do.

Reality: Most students have busy schedules and this program will require you to learn new concepts. However, the work of this program isn't reading a dozen additional books and writing more papers. The real work of the program is approaching the work that you do have differently. For instance, the ALC program will challenge and offer you a new way to study and approach the work that you do have in a different way. Applying these concepts will free more of your time and energy up to do what you love to do.

Myth #3: A coach is going to be a spy for my parents and is just going to get me to do what my parents want me to do.

Reality: A good coach rarely tells you directly what to do. The magic of coaching is that the client and coach design the action steps after each session together. You get to choose how you use the concepts in your life.

As outlined in the professional ethics of a Certified Life Coach, confidentiality is a central part of the coach/client relationship. If there is something you don't want your parents to know, your Certified Life Coach won't share it with your parents except in the rare circumstance that it is information about something that may harm you or others.

Academic Life Coaches are trained to help you get where you want to go and to help parents understand the best way they can support you. You get an opportunity to let your parents know the best way to interact with you in a way that you both benefit. The result is that you and your parents get more of what you both want: a peaceful and strong relationship.

Myth #4: Others will know that I have a Coach.

Reality: Most people don't care if others know they are working with a coach. But if you do care and don't want anyone else to know that you're working with a coach, your coach will respect your wish. A Certified Life Coach understands the confidentiality of the coach/client relationship and won't share with others that they are your coach or any of the information shared in a coaching relationship. You, however, are free to share with anyone you want that you are working with a coach as well as what you're learning.

Working with a coach is one of the best investments you can make of your time, energy, and resources. By far the best way to learn about coaching is to experience it. But before we jump in, here are some guidelines that will help make the program one of the highlights of your education.

Guidelines for the Academic Life Coaching Program

While there are no set "rules" for what helps and what doesn't in a coaching session, there are some guidelines that make a big difference in what you get out of the Academic Life Coaching program. At the center of the program is your relationship with your coach, your understanding of the concepts, and your ability to follow through with the exercises between sessions. The bottom-line is that the success of the program is up to you, and just like in life, you'll get about as much back as you put in.

Guideline #1: Trust Your Imagination.

Many of the questions your coach will ask you are designed to make you think about yourself and your situation differently. It's the coach's job to ask hard questions and questions that make you think deeply. Take your time and trust your imagination. Many of the exercises require that you take mini-leaps of faith in thinking about what's true for you, and your coach is trained to help you pick apart the fluff from what's real. Trust yourself and trust the process.

One way to look at school and the ALC program is thinking about the kinds of tests and quizzes you have to take. Generally speaking, there are two kinds of assessments: those where the right answer is known (like on a Math test), and those where the right answer is not yet known, but you know it when it clicks (like writing a fantastic college application essay). Many of the questions and exercises in the ALC program do not have "right" answers - and no one really knows the right answer for you - but in the process you'll discover an answer that works for you. To get there, you have to trust your imagination and go with it.

As you learn to trust your imagination and dream bigger, you'll not only realize how powerful your imagination can be but also how achievable your goals are.

Guideline #2: Get beyond Right/Wrong and Good/Bad.

The idea of right versus wrong and good versus bad often gets in the way and slows progress. Instead of thinking in those terms, I encourage you to get away from judgements. The words *right, wrong, good,* and *bad,* carry so much emotional baggage of judgement that it makes creating positive change and habits more challenging.

Instead of thinking in those terms, I encourage you to think in terms of things being useful, somewhat useful, and useless. Some habits are really useful. Some aren't. When you avoid thinking about something being good or bad and rather focus on the usefulness (or uselessness) it helps you make a positive choice without the extra step of dealing with the judgement and emotion of doing something "wrong" or "bad."

Guideline #3: Learn from Failure.

Failure is inevitable, not the big dismal crash and burn failure, but the little I'm-going-to-try-something-new-to-see-if-it-works-or-not failure is. Both kinds are useful for your long-term learning, although I'm a much bigger fan of the little I'm-going-to-try-something kind. In fact, if you aren't having failures, you're also not having as many meaningful successes in your life. The key to failure is to learn from it and recover quickly. The quicker you get back on form and move forward the better off you are. The skill to develop to deal with failure is resilience, how quickly you can recover, and adaptability - how quickly you can learn from your mistakes and be flexible to try something different.

Between sessions you'll inevitably do some of the exercises really well and be dismal on others. Your job is to fully apply yourself and go from uncertainty and practice to confidence and mastery. If you fail along the way, recover, and keep moving forward.

Guideline #4: There is No Neutral.

Sometimes we can get lulled into thinking that there are three speeds: forward, neutral, and reverse. In reality there are only two speeds, forward or reverse. If you aren't moving forward, then you're moving backwards. As long as you're fully applying yourself and looking for ways to improve your system, then you're doing your job regardless of the outcome. The key is to keep moving just a little faster than the demands of life, and when you don't, learn from it, dust yourself off, and keep on truckin'.

Academic Life Coaching Curriculum

The following pages will lead you through the exercises of the Academic Life Coaching Program. It's advisable to follow through the program in the order presented, although at times your coach will ask you to jump around in sessions, which often happens and is completely fine.

Session One (Academic Success, Part 1)

Wheel of Life

Well-Formed Outcomes

Learning Styles

Design the Coach/Client Alliance

Date:

Your Notes:

Your Agreed Action Steps:

Debrief (to be filled out during the week or at the beginning of next session)

What worked?

What didn't work?

What did you learn?

Notes:

Wheel of Life

The Wheel of Life is a popular life coaching exercise that gives clients a quick overview of their life. They identify areas they want to focus on, and get a great visual representation of progress made. In the Academic Life Coaching Program, we'll end up doing four Wheels of Life in the ten sessions.

How to Create and Use Your Own Wheel of Life

1) Draw a circle or use the one on the following page.
2) As if the circle were apple pie, draw four lines to cut the pie into eight pieces.
3) Determine the eight areas of your life you want to use. (The wheel that follows has been designed for students)
4) Write each label around the outer edge of the wheel.
    1) School: Your overall experience of being in class and being with your friends
    2) Grades: How happy (or not) you are with your grades
    3) Family: Usually your immediate family, and if you need to break this wedge into two (parents and siblings) that works
    4) Friends: Pretty straight forward
    5) Health: How healthy you feel, how much you exercise, and your diet
    6) Fun: How much fun you are having
    7) Room: How clean or messy your room is and how happy you are with it
    8) Growth: How you feel you are growing personally and spiritually
5) Then rate your *current level of satisfaction* for each area on a scale of one to ten, with ten being the highest.
6) Then for each wedge draw a line parallel to the circumference of the circle that represents the percentage of the pie piece that corresponds to your number. After you do this step, you should have a wheel drawn inside the circle that looks like it would a cog or gear.

Date:

Your coach will have some insightful questions to ask and perhaps an exercise that uses the wheel as a starting point. Here are a few questions to get you started:

Looking at your wheel, what jumps out at you?

If you were to choose just one wedge and do one action to increase that number from a 7 to an 8 (for instance), what would that action be?

Do you want to follow through with the action? If so, how will your coach know that you did so?

Save your wheels. I do this exercise with myself about once a quarter (every three months) and I date them. It's a great exercise to look back and see that *the action you take from doing this exercise really does make a difference in your life over the long-run.* So often your successes can get buried in the details of living that we forget what was the reality even three months ago. Consider this an exercise to make sure your life is balanced, a kick in the pants to get you moving, and a tool to remind you how far you've come.

Well-Formed Outcomes

Goals are Overrated

When people think about Life Coaching and improving their life, goals is one of the first words that comes to mind. "You need to have some goals," is said too often. On the one hand, having goals are great. But unfortunately, the word *goal* is overused. The concept of having 'SMART' goals gets closer to being useful, but the whole process of setting goals and then trying really hard to get them (often doing the same actions just harder) usually leads to frustration.

The Virtue of a Well-Formed Outcome

Instead of creating goals, it's much more effective to think in terms of creating a system that leads to an outcome. The *well-formed* part of a well-formed outcome refers to the characteristics of the end result that help focus the mind and attention in a way that boosts natural, intrinsic motivation. It will help you learn the valuable skill of moving forward when you most need to move.

The *outcome* part of a well-formed outcome refers to thinking in terms of systems, not simply in terms of effort and reward. Outcomes can happen naturally, sometimes with little or no effort. (Goals always require effort.) Outcomes are usually part of a system. If you can learn to create systems that work effectively, you will be astonished at how much you can achieve.

A well-formed outcome meets these criteria:
   1) Stated in the positive
   2) Getting started and the success (or failure) of the outcome depends entirely on you
   3) It has a good size to time ratio that moves you into action and keeps you moving at a comfortable pace
   4) It is specific and measurable

Here are a few popular examples of goals turned into well-formed outcomes:

Goal: To get all A's
Well-formed outcome: To study for all my tests for one hour or more TWO days before the test date.

Goal: To not get a bad grade
Well-formed outcome: To write in my planner each class, and if I don't have any homework I'll write "no homework"

Goal: To not get yelled at by my parents
Well-formed outcome: To ask my parents to do something fun this weekend

---

The biggest virtue of the well-formed outcome is that they empower you with full control of the success or failure of the outcome. So much of our lives falls outside our control. Most goals involve a high degree of stuff that needs to happen that also fall outside our control. For example, it's impossible to control the grade that you may get on an essay. Yet so many students have a goal to get good grades.

A well-formed outcome, on the other hand, will focus you on the actual process of writing your paper effectively and in a way that produces their best work. Learning is to turn their attention inward and focus on what you can control in your life and to follow through on that action, which is one of most valuable skills young people can acquire. The concept of a well-formed outcome helps students learn - and practice - that crucial skill.

Achieving any of these well-formed outcomes doesn't automatically mean that you will get all A's, avoid bad grades and being yelled at by your parents. However, following through on the outcomes over time does make a big difference in your self-confidence, ability to create new habits, and eventually the results that you will get.

I often see students who start to apply the concept of a well-formed outcome, take the outcome and incorporate into their life so fully that they forget that they even set it as an outcome weeks ago. The well-formed outcome has become a habit, and they are off to creating the next outcome and system.

Throughout the Academic Life Coaching Program, you'll create many well-formed outcomes with your coach, and being able to create and set them for yourself is a crucial skill to being fulfilled and effective.

Now it's time for you to write out some of your own well-formed outcomes with the help of your coach.

#1:

What structure or system do you need that will help make this outcome easy to accomplish?

What will let you know that you've accomplished this outcome?

#2:

What structure or system do you need that will help make this outcome easy to accomplish?

What will let you know that you've accomplished this outcome?

#3:

What structure or system do you need that will help make this outcome easy to accomplish?

What will let you know that you've accomplished this outcome?

B-

This is not a test
of my **grades**e.
It serves only to
help me improve
are study system
I am n**not**my
grades. I won't
let **Judgement!**
get me down!

Learning Styles: Visual, Audio, Kinesthetic

The grades you earn are not a reflection of your intelligence. They are a reflection of the system and habits that you use to learn. If you change your system, you will change the outcome. The next two concepts - Learning and Academic Thinking Styles - are designed to help you think about school and your classes differently.

Learnings styles is a vast topic. Many books have been written about the different kinds of styles and what are the best approaches to learning. When the Academic Life Coaching program was being created, I tried many different systems of learning styles. I found the most effective tools were the simplest, and keeping a focus on just three different modes of thinking and processing information was the best. Those three learning style mimic our senses: seeing (visual), hearing (audio), and touch (kinesthetic).

Because the Academic Life Coaching Program is a *life coaching* program, it's important that the information about learning styles is assimilated into action as well as designed jointly by the coach and you. Your Academic Life Coach will have some specific suggestions for how to best integrate learning styles into a study method, and it's up to you to co-design the exercises to build your learning styles as well as integrate them into your study habits with your coach.

A common question is whether certain learning styles are better than others. The answer is, 'Yes.' It can be unfortunate, but certain learning styles are better suited for academic success. A visual learning style is the strongest academically, followed by audio, and trailed by kinesthetic. If your strongest learning style is either audio or kinesthetic, it's best if you develop that style as well as strengthen your visual prowess.

How to Determine Your Learning Style

The following quiz is designed to give you a quick picture of your Visual-Audio-Kinesthetic Profile. Simply circle the letter to the phrase that best completes each sentence. Trust your first response. Then use the chart that follows to tally your responses.

Learning Styles Quiz

1. I know something is right when:
   a) It looks right.
   b) It sounds right.
   c) It feels right.

2. When I have to make something, I like to:
   a) Jump right in and figure it out as I go.
   b) Look at the pictures in the instructions.
   c) Read the instructions and explanations.

3. When I'm in a new city, to find my way around I like to:
   a) Study a map.
   b) Ask for directions.
   c) Walk around to get a feeling for where things are.

4. When I'm showing someone how to do something, I like to:
   a) Do it first then turn it over to them.
   b) Talk them through it.
   c) Point out what they need to pay attention to.

5. When I choose something from a menu, I like to:
   a) Read the choices and visualize what I want.
   b) Have someone read the specials of the day and pick what sounds good.
   c) Follow the feeling in my stomach.

6. When I absolutely need to concentrate, I like to:
   a) Have something in my hands I can fiddle with as I'm thinking.
   b) Be still and focus on what's in front of me.
   c) Talk it through in my head.

7. When I'm remembering how to spell a difficult word, I usually:

    a)   Picture it in my head.

    b)   Hear myself say the letters in order.

    c)   Have to write it down.

8. When I'm worried about something, I usually:

    a)   Talk it over with myself, and try to ignore the record playing in my head.

    b)   Picture the worst that could happen but try to "fix" the picture.

    c)   Move around and not be still.

9. When I speak in front of a group, I am most comfortable when:

    a)   There's room where I can walk around and gesture freely.

    b)   I can hear my voice calm and confident in the opening and closing.

    c)   I have a powerpoint presentation or other visual aids set up.

10.   When I'm really happy about something about to happen, I usually:

    a)   See a picture of how great it's going to be.

    b)   Talk to myself to psych myself up.

    c)   Feel an extra burst of energy and not sit still.

In the chart below circle your response to each sentence. Then tally up your responses.

Sentence Number	Visual	Audio	Kinesthetic
1	a	b	c
2	b	c	a
3	a	b	c
4	c	b	a
5	a	b	c
6	b	c	a
7	a	b	c
8	b	a	c
9	c	b	a
10	a	b	c
Totals			

Primary learning style:

Secondary learning style:

Here are a few recommendations for exercises that will stretch and strengthen your learning styles:

Visual
- When reading go straight to creating a picture in your head.
- Draw a quick sketch of the picture when studying.
- Spell words in their mind's eye forwards and backwards.
- Practice taking a perfect "snap shot" of the information then recreating it on a blank sheet of paper.

Audio
- Make up funny ways to say important words or information. Rhyming and alliteration are great.
- Create a quick verbal summary of the information.
- Say it out loud or write it down. The act of creating speech is a great way for audio learners to study.

Kinesthetic
- Flashcards are key, especially the act of making flashcards helps so much. (Really flashcards are good for each learning style, but especially kinesthetic learners).
- Take notes. By engaging in movement, kinesthetic learners are better able to understand the material.
- When reading scan through the material quickly, then go back and pick up the details.

Exercises you want to use to leverage strengths:

Exercises you want to use to develop weaker learning styles:

Design the Client-Coach-Parent Alliance

Throughout the coaching, we have the opportunity to design the relationship in a way that best serves you. To do so, it's helpful to think of what motivates you best (more heart or heat from your coach), how you move into action, what requests you have, what you think I should know, what's working, what's not working, and how will you know this coaching has been successful.

What best motivates you?

How do you move into action?

What requests do you have?

What do you think I should know?

What's working so far?

What's not working so far?

How will you know that this coaching has been successful?

What's the best way to communicate what you're accomplishing to your parents?

Session Two (Academic Success, Part 2)

Study Skills: Academic Thinking Styles
Core Motivation
Motivation Styles

Motivation Matters

Date:

Your Notes:

Your Agreed Action Steps:

Debrief (to be filled out during the week or at the beginning of next session)

What worked?

What didn't work?

What did you learn?

Notes:

Thinking Styles

Just like learning styles, thinking styles are different for everyone. One of the benefits of looking at thinking styles, especially in the context of a life coaching program, is that knowing your thinking style is another tool to succeed that you can tailor to your specific process of learning. It's another way of understanding what makes you unique., it increases your self-awareness., and it helps you understand why some teachers style makes sense while others don't.

The grades that you receive

Here's an excerpt from an essay in *Future-Proofed* that addresses Thinking Styles:

The brain is a thinking machine. Just as everyone has a specific style of speaking, the brain has a specific style of thinking. From one point-of-view the brain can be thought of as an information device. It's designed to gather information about the environment to keep you safe from danger and alert to opportunities.

Your thinking style is going to be approaching the knowledge from many different points of view. The problem occurs when students think that they know a topic, but really, they just know one perspective of the topic. They just know the details, the definitions, and not necessarily how everything fits together or connects. For example, students may know how to do a math problem but they may not necessarily know why it works or what it's called.

When you know your thinking style, you'll know your strength and you'll also know what thinking styles you need to develop. Ideally, you will become comfortable in each of the three thinking styles. You will get in the habit of taking notes with each question answered for each concept, and include each thinking style in your writing.

As such, your brain focuses on 3 specific questions to make sense of the world.

1) What?
2) Why?
3) How?

WHAT WHY WHY HOW THINK!

How to Find Your Thinking Style

Your Academic Life Coach will provide a lot of valuable experience to help you determine your Thinking Style. Sometimes your style is readily apparent. Sometimes, it's tough to determine. The key is to recognize the kinds of questions you find yourself asking when trying to learn something. Here are three paragraphs about characteristics of each thinking style.

What Thinkers

What-thinkers tend to love detail and want to know the names, definitions, facts, and more about the material itself. What-thinkers may put a copious number of facts in an essay, and put hours of work into their writing, but be frustrated with not earning the highest grade because teachers want more analysis. (In other words, the teachers want to know more than just the facts and have a balance of thinking styles in an essay.) What-thinkers assume that if they can know all the correct facts, and are knowledgable about the facts of a situation, the cause (or why) or method (or how) will be apparent.

Why Thinkers

Why-thinkers want to understand the reasons behind the action. Detail is somewhat important, but not as important as knowing the motivation behind someone doing something or the cause of something happening. These kinds of learners tend to drive what-teachers crazy, especially in a subject like Math. Why-thinkers assume that if they can know the causes behind something, they know all the important facts and there can be any number of methods to accomplish it.

How Thinkers

How thinkers want to understand how they can do something or how it happened. To a how-thinker, most details aren't that important, but the essential details are paramount. When writing how-thinkers tend to summarize or retell the event *from their particular point-of-view*. As a result their papers tend to be light on synopsis and analysis and make the reader work to fill in many of the details. How-thinkers assume that the reasons are obvious, the details are usually superfluous, yet if someone knows how to do something, all the other pieces of knowledge will fall into place.

How to Use the Concept of Thinking Styles

Each Thinking Style is a channel or method of thought. Each is valid and important. Similar to a learning style, one of the goals of knowing about and using thinking styles is to become proficient at each style as well as know which styles might be your weak point. If you know, for instance, that you are a how-thinker, you may want to take more time focusing on the specific definitions or names when studying. If you are a what-thinker, you may want to spend more time looking for analysis and the reasons behind action. If you are a why-thinker, it would be worthwhile to spend just a little more time on the names and definitions as well as get used to learning specific methods for solving a problem.

The key to using learning styles is to become comfortable with each style, and to make sure that when you are studying you understand the concept from each of the three angles.

1) What are the details and definitions?
2) Why did it happen this way? Why does it work?
3) How did it happen? How can I do it?

Exercises for building your Thinking Styles:

1) Take notes that you would usually take in class. Then, when reviewing your notes, code them into What, Why, and How for each major concept. If you can't find a Why or How, that's a good question to ask the teacher next time in class.

2) Practice writing paragraphs that address each of the four questions. Students often find themselves favoring one thinking style, which leads to writing that's either filled with too many details and little analysis, or a summary of what happened without really letting the reader know what the main topic is and the reasons behind it. By addressing each of the four thinking styles, in turn, you ensure that you will begin to write outstanding paragraphs and papers (which will also help you on the college application).

3) Pay attention to the kinds of questions each teacher asks and the kinds of information your teacher is giving in class. Is your teacher fond of names, dates, and details? If so, then she's probably a 'what-thinker.' Does he like to delve into the possible reasons why something happens? Then he's a 'why-thinker.' Does she spend a lot of time going step-by-step through the problem or section? Then she's probably a 'how-thinker.'

Core Motivation

Finding what really motivates you is a tremendous tool in helping you overcome challenges and do the work that most needs to be done. It's also a tool to develop your self-awareness and gain a better understanding of how to take advantage of your personality's strengths and manage it's weaknesses.

As with any personality system, especially one that considers what really motivates you there is the concern that a system can't possibly be descriptive and give an accurate picture of the richness of your personality or uniquiness of you as an individual. The concern is valid, and the core motivation tools is designed merely to give you a clearer insight into factors that could possibly influence patterns in the way that you think and habits in how you get yourself motivated. The tool also points to the natural strengths of your core motivation as well as usual blind-spots that limit and hinder your success.

The tool will also offer suggestions on the natural strengths of your core motivation when communicating and when leading. It will also suggest exercises that will encourage you to develop stronger communication skills and become a more effective leader.

Here are the guidelines:
- To find your core motivation, simply read the nine paragraphs below. The paragraphs describe each of the nine different kinds of motivation.
- Everyone has a little of each core motivation. And in different parts of our lives we can rely on different motivations. A few paragraphs will seem to fit.
- However, when we get down to what really motivates us, one core style will stand out.
- To find your style, read the nine following paragraphs and chose the top one or two that best describe you.
- Your coach will help guide you to determine which of the nine styles fits best.
- After you determine your style, your coach will help you learn more details about your core motivation and integrate what you have learned into the Academic Life Coaching program.

The Core Motivation Paragraphs

Type One: The Perfectionist

I strive for things to be perfect and in place. If I'm passionate about something, I work really hard and spend a lot of time on it. I want other things around me to be perfect, but I am mostly hard on myself. I am very critical of the things I do and I am very disappointed in myself when I make a mistake. I often have a lot of priorities on my plate, but I just want to improve my life and the lives of others. Often times people follow my lead and I am comfortable in that leadership capacity. Whatever I have to do, it has to be done right and I will do what it takes to get there. Others might say I am intense or too serious at times, but I just like to be focused and I would rather relax when the work is done.

Type Two: The Helper

What really drives me is my ability to help others. I love doing things for somebody, especially if I know they will appreciate it. I feel like I know how best to help people because it's usually easy for me to determine their wants and needs. It might seem like I try too hard or am controlling at times, but it's just because I want to help in the best way. I get satisfaction out of putting others before myself, though sometimes that takes it toll when I don't focus on my own needs. I like when others recognize that I am there for them and I usually have a difficult time saying 'no.' I also place a huge emphasis on relationships. I give a lot of myself in hopes that others will recognize what I have given, and in turn will respect me for that. At the end of the day I hope that the people I help will be there for me when necessary.

Type Three: The Doer

I want to be the best I can be at what I do. Goals are important to me and I work hard at achieving them. I feel very successful when I meet my goals, and I want others to respect me for it. My mind works rather quickly and sometimes I can get irritable if something or someone seems to be working too slowly. Though I am personally competitive, I can also do well on a team and am well liked. I want to make a good impression on people and I care about how others view me. When I have a really passionate goal, I know just what to do to achieve it and stay motivated. I prefer to do only the things I am good at.

Type Four: The Artist

I like to express my emotions and I want others to understand me for who I am. I consider myself genuine and unique. I'm constantly seeking more in terms of my life and I try to evaluate and consider what is missing. I don't like to be misunderstood and sometimes people might mistake me for being dramatic or caring too much, but really I just want to express exactly how I feel. I like to get to know others on a deeper level and form real connections. I'm passionate about feelings and I want to accurately reveal myself to others.

Type Five: The Thinker

I love being the expert. Before I delve into something, I want to know as much as I can. I don't like to be wrong or corrected, which is why if I don't know something, I would rather not say it. I am happy to argue my points for what I believe is right, but if the facts don't support my idea, I will reconsider my idea. I often thrive on alone time and I like to think about my past experiences. I am pretty independent and I don't want to have to rely or depend on someone else. I crave information and knowledge and I am not shy in a group setting, where I can speak up and say what I know and express what I want. Overall, I am a simple person and my life is rather straightforward.

Type Six: The Friend

I like to be prepared for the worst. Often I envision worst-case scenarios so that I know just what to do in case they actually happen. I have a creative imagination and a somewhat odd sense of humor. I can be unsure of people in authority, especially if I don't trust them. Once I trust someone and have explored an idea, I will be very loyal. When it comes to new ideas, the first thing that usually comes to mind is what could go wrong. I would rather think it through before accepting it for face value. I am not much of a follower, especially when it comes to ideas, because I can easily pick out why I disagree with it.

Type Seven: The Optimist

I enjoy life at a fast pace. I like to create many options for myself and future plans and keep many options open. I shy away from negative emotion and I hate feeling bored or trapped with my life. If I am upset over something, I don't want to dwell on it. Sometimes I will get really excited over something rather quickly but then eventually I will get bored with it and forget about it or drop it. Often times I will start things that don't quite get finished. At the same time, I am very optimistic and I believe life is a ride that is meant to be enjoyed. When I have several options that I can choose from, I have a hard time deciding because I want them all.

Type Eight: The Defender

I like to be in control as much as possible. I am very blunt and honest because I want the things to be clear. It frustrates me when I feel like someone is conniving or unfair. At times I might seem controlling but I just want to take charge and keep things going smoothly. I try to hide my weaknesses because I feel vulnerable when someone else knows what they are. That being said, I think we should still recognize our weaknesses and do something about them. I would rather get something done on my own than be told what to do, which is why I sometimes have a hard time following orders from authority. I won't always respect a person of authority upfront, but when I do, I am much more willing to follow directions from them.

Type Nine: The Peacemaker

I like things to be peaceful and happy. I tend to avoid conflict and confrontation. Sometimes I can't even recognize exactly what I want so I just go with the flow, especially in group settings. When I do know what I want, I might still agree with someone even if it goes against that. I might get angry at myself, but I don't like getting angry at other people, or when people are angry at each other. I have a kind heart and I know it can be taken advantage of. When I really need to I know how to stand up for myself. I am good at seeing multiple sides to a situation, both pros and cons.

Challenges to and Exercises for Personal Growth

Challenges to personal growth	Exercises that aid personal growth
Type 1: The Perfectionist Being too hard on myself. Being too serious. Not taking time for myself for fun and pure enjoyment. Demanding perfection and not accepting every part of myself.	Improvisation and activities like improv are outstanding for 1's. They let ones act without getting stuck in their thoughts. Taking time out of the day for fun and laughter.
Type 2: The Helper Doing so much for others that I forget to take care of my needs. Becoming too involved in relationships. Becoming demanding when I am not recognized.	Write out what you want for each area of your life and becoming clear on the balance you want to achieve. Set aside time to treat yourself as you would another person.
Type 3: The Doer Realizing that your worth is who you are, not what you have accomplished. Sacrificing personal relationships for the sake of a goal.	Relax your focus on success and put your focus on what would fulfill you. Clarifying your values and what's really important to you.
Type 4: The Artist Over identifying with emotion, especially sad emotion, without moving into action. Resisting change if it is not dramatic. Feeling unworthy. Focusing too much on yourself.	Practice changing perspectives and choosing those perspectives that empower you to get what you really want. Create a positive vision of your future life.
Type 5: The Thinker Over-analyzing and being stubborn. Avoiding people or opportunities that seem to overwhelming. Being extremely private. Not moving into action.	Meditation. Especially short meditation during the day to check in with your emotions. Then move into action! You must act on what you decide.

Type 6: The Friend Not trusting yourself or others. Thinking about worst-case scenarios. Wanting to keep knowing more before making a decision. Doubt.	Check in with fear. Practice changing perspectives and choosing those that move you forward in a positive direction. Positive affirmations work for 6's.
Type 7: The Optimist Thinking that something they don't have will be better than what they have. Constant trying to avoid pain and not meeting responsibilities. Being distracted from bigger goals.	Clarify a mission statement and take small action steps to accomplish it. Meditation is very important to 7s. Exercise discipline.
Type 8: The Defender Being stubborn. Denying weakness and sensitivity. Fighting any attempt to be controlled and trying to control others. Acting in ways that make success harder to accomplish.	Focus on the gift that you can give to others. Listen closely to others and practice empathy. Resist being stubborn and constantly resisting others. When healthy 8's integrate to 2.
Type 9: The Peacemaker Ignoring problems and trying to be comfortable always. Not meeting problems when they first start and avoiding conflict at any cost. Not knowing what you really want.	Clarify a mission statement and commit to taking small action steps. Practice asserting yourself and saying 'no' to small things. Refuse to be passive-aggressive. Instead be assertive.

My Primary Core Motivation:

Challenges most apt to you:

How you know you're doing well:

Exercises for Personal Growth:

Motivation Styles

Life Coaching is designed to get you moving into action. Much of the magic in coaching comes from sparking motivation to do things differently. Harnessing motivation can be a challenge, but it's also one of the key skills for young people to master to lead an effective life.

The purpose of this section is to help you become more aware of the kinds of motivation available, and the characteristics, strengths, and weaknesses of each type of motivation.

The Academic Life Coaching Program looks at three distinctions in motivation styles to give you a better understanding of the factors of motivation and yourspecific mix that works best for them.

Those three factors are:

1) Conditional vs. Intrinsic
2) Away from Bad Stuff vs. Toward Good Stuff
3) Sake of Self vs. Other

In the Academic Life Coaching Program, it's essential to know and understand the different kinds of motivation and motivation styles. Especially with teenagers, who are just forming the styles they will use the most, knowing the different kinds of motivation can set a high school student up to succeed the rest of their academic career.

Once you are more aware of the different kinds and styles of motivation, you can more consciously tap into those that work the best for them. The outcomes are becoming more self-aware, confidence that you can get yourself moving when you need to, and less stressed because you are both kinder to themselves and actually excited to get the work done that needs to get done.

Conditional vs. Intrinsic Motivation

Conditional motivation is being motivated to do something for the sake of an external benefit. It's when people think, "If I do this, then I get this reward." Or it could be "If I don't do this, this won't happen." Anytime someone uses a conditional sentence - a pair of *if-then* clauses - he or she is using conditional motivation.

Intrinsic motivation is being motivated to do something because the action itself is the reward. It's when someone thinks, "I want to do this because it's fun." Or it could be, "I enjoy the challenge." Or even, "I want to see what happens when I follow through with..." Intrinsic motivation is about enjoying the process as much as the result.

While conditional motivation works well in the short-term, to be successful in school without much of the stress, it's important to find a way to be intrinsically motivated. In other words, you must find a way to balance doing your homework for the sake of the grade with doing your homework because learning and doing the work is enjoyable.

I'm sure you've had the experience of being on top of your work and doing an assignment and actually enjoying it. It's natural, the brain wants to learn. Finding that place again when learning is fun allows you to take more control of your motivation so you can switch between conditional (for short bursts of energy) and intrinsic (to be your main engine) at will.

The biggest key in shifting to a more intrinsic form of motivation, which is going to be more useful to you over the long-run, is simply being aware of which motivation style you are using. Your awareness goes a long way to determining which style you use. Once you find the joy of tapping into an intrinsic style of motivation, it quickly becomes a positive habit.

When do you find yourself using Conditional Motivation?

For which activities do you naturally use Intrinsic Motivation?

In your school work, what's your balance between Conditional and Intrinsic Motivation?

What could you do to shift that balance slightly more in the direction of Intrinsic Motivation?

Motivation Away from Bad Stuff vs. Toward Good Stuff

There are two primary ways to get you moving:

1) Moving away from what you want to avoid.
2) Going toward what you want to get.

The first chart is an example of being motivated AWAY from what you don't want. It could be a bad grade (which could be a D, C, or B - or even an A-) or being yelled at by your parents. Really anything that you don't want to happen serves as a good source of motivation.

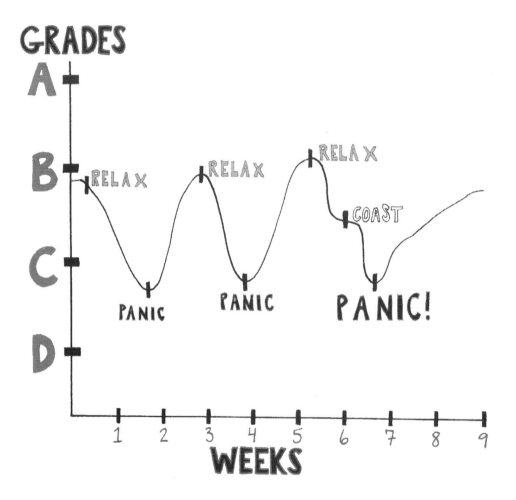

The second chart is an example of being motivated toward what you do want to happen. Notice how it may be difficult to get moving at first because you are so far away from your primary source of motivation. Once you get closer to the outcome you want, you start to pick up pace because you can see how close you are and the experience of what you really want becomes more real.

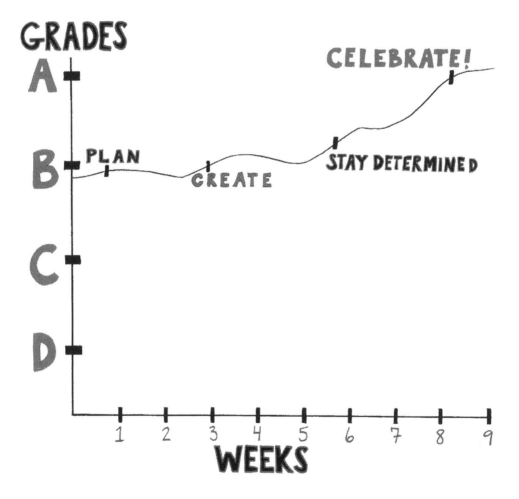

In school, what's your usual balance between being motivated 'Away From' versus 'Towards'?

What areas of your life do you find yourself using an 'Away From' motivation style?

What areas of your life do you find yourself using a 'Towards' motivation style?

Motivation for the Sake of Self vs. Other

Here's a chart for you to map out the pain and the benefits that happen when you achieve the outcome you want as well as add what will happen in your own life and in the lives of others when you follow through.

Note: When thinking about the impact in the lives of others, it's not necessary to have an answer. It can be difficult to think about the benefit of what getting all A's and B's will be on your family 20 years from now. However, it's still useful to think about the impact on how your decisions now will affect the future.

Outcome you want:

	Bad Stuff if you don't follow through	Good Stuff if you do follow through
In My Life		
In the Lives of Others (for instance your parents or friends)		
In the World and Others I don't yet know (for instance the impact your of your career)		

Session Three (Academic Success, Part 3)

Vision
Systems, Thinking, and Organization
Structures and Anchors
Recipe for Academic Success

√Systems

Date:

Your Notes:

Your Agreed Action Steps:

Debrief (to be filled out during the week or at the beginning of next session)

What worked?

What didn't work?

What did you learn?

Notes:

Vision, Creating a Tape/Structure to Make it Real

In the last session we reviewed the importance of having a vision in mind to keep you motivated towards an outcome. In this session, you get the opportunity to create a reminder for that vision for you to work towards. The more details you can add to your vision, the richer and more useful it will be for you.

Start with another Wheel of Life, but this time, instead of putting what's currently happening, put what you ideally want in each of the wedges.

Then imagine yourself in a year (or some other time in the future). From the point of view of the future, look back on what you have accomplished and write about your life as if that amazing outcome is real and you have lived that reality.

Recipe for Academic Success

This is a short little gut check to make sure that you're doing what you need to do to succeed academically. If you're not getting the grades you want, or you're stressed out trying to get those grades and working too hard, you're not doing one of these three things:

1) Using your learning and academic thinking style when taking notes and studying.
2) Using your planner and systems binder.
3) Talking to your teachers about what you can do better.

Most students do two out of the three. Which one do you need to work on?

When will you work on it?

How will you know that your action is contributing to your success?

What other area in your life have you experienced success?

What made success easy for you?

How can you incorporate the same values/beliefs/actions to how you approach school and your grades?

Systems and Organization

You've just created a vision for where you want to go in your life, and you're also more aware of the three ingredients to be successful academically. Now it's time to find a way to make that vision - and your ongoing academic success - reality.

The best way to accomplish such an undertaking is to create a system that's sustainable and designed to fit you. The key is to work first on the system, then to do the work. The mistake most students make is simply diving in and doing the work and without thinking about the best way to do it in the future or designing a way to stay on top of all their work all the time.

Without a system, most people bounce between being completely on top of things (like having a clean room, binder and all their work finished) to being behind (a messy room, stuffed binder, and a few missing assignments). With a system there are sure to be times when things get hectic, but you're able to handle a bigger workload without feeling the stress. A great system is the key to doing well in school and avoiding most of the stress associated with being a student.

The other key is to look at creating a system where the stuff (for example: your binder, your notes, your planner, your desk, etc.) aligns with what you need to do and what wants to happen naturally. Here's an example that illustrates the point:

Back in 2005 I was working with a student who was helplessly disorganized. It was March but he had papers stuffed in his binder from the beginning of the school year, and they weren't just the class syllabus. He had actual quizzes and old homework assignments crunched in between the rings and in the bottom of his backpack. His parents thought it was no use, and since he was getting good grades, they left him alone. The only problem was that he was super stressed out anytime he had to find something and the level of stress was starting to get to him.

We looked at what he had and what he was trying to accomplish and we decided that he only needed to do five things with any piece of paper he was handed. He had to do it as homework, turn it back into the teacher, study, file, or get rid of it. To mimic the actions he needed to take, he created a binder with five folders and labeled each folder with the action. He did NOT immediately clean out his binder all at once. Instead he let his system work for a week, and what he found was that he was naturally cleaning out his backpack and class binders because he had the confidence that he really didn't need many of the papers in there. It was a slow natural progression, and even weeks later (and years later) he still used the system to keep on top of his work.

His system:

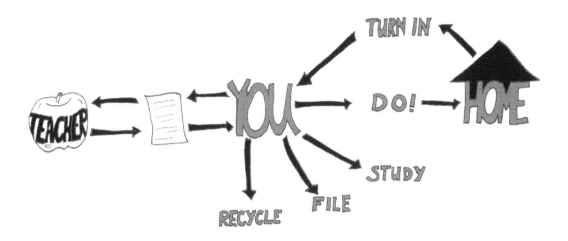

The *paper* is the *raw material*. The *you* is the *choice point*. And the *arrows* and *actions* are the *structure* of the system.

Now it's your turn to create your own system. The first part is to get clear on what you want to accomplish. Then it's on the fun part of creating a process that seamlessly takes you from your starting point and raw ingredients to your final product (while avoiding most of the mess).

Desired Outcome:

Inputs/Raw Ingredients:

What's currently working? (This gives you great clues on what you can build on.)

What's NOT currently working? (This gives you great clues on the structures you need.)

Decision Points: Determine the point you have to make the decision to do something with the raw materials (it will inform the kind of structures you need)

Structures: Align what you have to *do* with *binders, bins, folders, planners or whatever* you need to mimic the action you need to take

Diagram of your system:

Dropping Anchors

You just created a system and put in place some structures to keep things in order. The final step is to create a few anchors. You can view an anchor as a mental structure designed to get your mind back in the game when something knocks you off track. Usual anchors are words, specific movements, and images that you've designated to remind you to get back in the game. If you have a solid structure and a few anchors to help you recover quickly, you'll find it easy to move forward at a steady, effective pace.

Your coach will help you drop a few of your own anchors, and as you go through the next three sessions in the *Academic Life Coaching Program*, you'll have material to create some of your own.

Well-Formed Outcome, Motivation, or System your anchor is used for:

Specific Anchor:

What it reminds you of:

Well-Formed Outcome, Motivation, or System your anchor is used for:

Specific Anchor:

What it reminds you of:

Session Four (Personal Fluency Part 1)

Assumptions

Beliefs

Perspectives

Core Motivation Part 2

Date:

Your Notes:

Your Agreed Action Steps:

Debrief (to be filled out during the week or at the beginning of next session)

What worked?

What didn't work?

What did you learn?

Notes:

Assumption Chart

This chart helps you get unstuck and stop spending energy working against yourself. It works because it gets to the root of the problem: the assumptions you make about yourself, an area of your life, or a task your trying to accomplish.

Assumptions quickly lead to perspectives, which influence the action taken. Those three - assumptions, perspectives, and action - determine the outcome which becomes evidence to support the original assumption.

As human beings we want our assumptions to be proven true, even if they go against what we want. The reason: it's extremely stressful to be inaccurate about beliefs about ourselves and the world. Here's your chance to align what you want with your underlying assumptions and spend your resources wisely.

Negative Assumption:

Assumption (Leads to Perspective)	Evidence (Leads back to Assumption)
Perspective (Leads to Action)	Action (Leads to Evidence)

Positive Assumption:

Assumption (Leads to Perspective)	Evidence (Leads back to Assumption)
Perspective (Leads to Action)	Action (Leads to Evidence)

Busting Limiting Beliefs

Limiting beliefs are easy to bust when you get into the habit of recognizing them. The key is to recognize areas in which you are struggling and determine what underlying beliefs you have about yourself or the tasks that are not helpful. Once identified, you can use the assumption chart - or this quicker, more to-the-point busting limiting beliefs exercise - to realign your beliefs to best serve you.

Tough area/Results not what you want

Beliefs about Yourself/Task

Circle helpful beliefs
Cross out limiting beliefs

It may be a stretch or easy for you to switch out the opposite of a limiting belief, but when you do choose an empowering belief you start to look for the evidence that it's true. You're ability to build on what's working is a great skill to have in your tool belt.

Write the opposite of limiting beliefs below.

Write out what different actions you'd take based on positive beliefs.

Signature Perspectives

Throughout our day we often slip into many different perspectives about the tasks that we are trying to undertake. The key here is to find the most empowering perspective and use it as your signature perspective: that perspective that is uniquely yours, fits you best, and becomes your signature for the way you look at life.

Focus:

Perspective #1:

Perspective #2:

Perspective #3:

Perspective #4:

Most empowering perspective:

What's possible from this perspective:

Cues to remind you of the perspective:

Core Motivation Check-Up

The main benefit of knowing your core motivation is being able to separate it from you. Although your core motivation makes up an essential part of your personality, you are not your personality alone. Your personality is a bundle of thoughts, beliefs, and actions that make you up. Once you have the ability to see your personality and manage it, you're able to account for your tendencies, break habits that you no longer want, and create habits that will best serve you.

Strengths of your core motivation:

Weaknesses of your core motivation:

When you know you're doing really well:

When you know that you're in trouble:

How you recover back to an empowered perspective:

Session Five (Personal Fluency Part 2)

Trademarked Values

Making Decisions

Future-Pacing

Self-Alignment: Getting Over Jet-Lag

Date:

Your Notes:

Your Agreed Action Steps:

Debrief (to be filled out during the week or at the beginning of next session)

What worked?

What didn't work?

What did you learn?

Notes:

Trademarked Values

Value comes from the Latin word *valere* meaning to be strong or fare well. Values are literally those things in our lives that fortify us and are of worth. They are unique to each of us. This exercise is designed to help you recognize your top five values and treat them like they are your trademark, the unique values that help define you. Once you clarify those values and find ways to include more of them in your life you will be on the path to fulfillment.

Value #1:

Description:

Value #2:

Description:

Value #3:

Description:

Value #4:

Description:

Value #5:

Description:

Making Decisions

Now it's time to put your values into action, especially when it comes time for you to make decisions. To make informed decisions, you have to know what's most important to you. Your values can help guide your decisions, especially when you can pull out what's most important to you and consciously include more of it in your life.

An area of your life you want to focus on:

Value that you want to honor in that area:

The actual point in that system when you make a decision to follow through on your value:

Systems and structures you have in place to support you:

Other insights:

Future-Pacing

Future-pacing has two steps. The first, imagining yourself in the future, making the choice you want to make or having your life go the way you want it to go. The second is continuing to imagine the scene as if it were a movie. In essence you are pacing your mind through your vision in the future. Thus the name, future-pacing.

You can also use future-pacing to imagine that point in your future where you've achieved your outcome and then pace backwards (as if watching a movie in rewind) to the present moment.

This exercise with its two variations is similar to the visioning exercise with the main difference that future-pacing places its focus on turning your vision into a movie and sticking with the vision. It's a great exercise for you to develop your imagination and push its limits.

Here's some space for you to write out some notes for your vision:

Self-Alignment: Getting Over Jet-Lag

It's like taking yourself to the Chiropractor. You have to get realigned every so often, especially when you're making the kind of big change that you've been making over the past weeks.

Using the Wheel of Life, take a value or a new system that you've created and look at the impact it has on all the other areas of your life.

Have your coach lead you back through, reinforcing the work that you've done and the progress that you've made.

Session Six (Personal Fluency, Part 3)

Inner-Critic

Future-Self

Date:

Your Notes:

Your Agreed Action Steps:

Debrief (to be filled out during the week or at the beginning of next session)

What worked?

What didn't work?

What did you learn?

Notes:

Inner-Critic

Your inner-critic is the negative self-talk, images, and feelings that we evoke. In this exercise you use your imagination to separate yourself from this not-so-helpful pattern.

What kinds of things do you say to yourself when doing poorly?

If you were to imagine someone else saying this to you, who/what would it look like?

What would its name be?

How big or small?

Other physical description (for example, what kind of clothes)?

It's mission?

When does it show up most often?

Short Biography:

Future-Self

Your future-self is your vision of yourself 10 to 15 years in the future. Your coach will lead you through a visualization and exercises for you to meet your future-self. Once you do so, you can use the prompts below to get an even clearer picture of your future-self.

Future-self's nickname:

Fashion style:

Geographic location:

Description of home:

Occupation:

Typical day:

Favorite things to do:

Top values:

Message to you:

Other notes:

Session Seven (Personal Leadership, Part 1)

Assumptions in Relationships

Empathy

we are
all on
the
same
team

Date:

Your Notes:

Your Agreed Action Steps:

Debrief (to be filled out during the week or at the beginning of next session)

What worked?

What didn't work?

What did you learn?

Notes:

Powerful Relationships

Relationships are central to living a fulfilling life. You can use the following chart below to check your assumptions, diagram how relationships are not working, and get back on the right track.

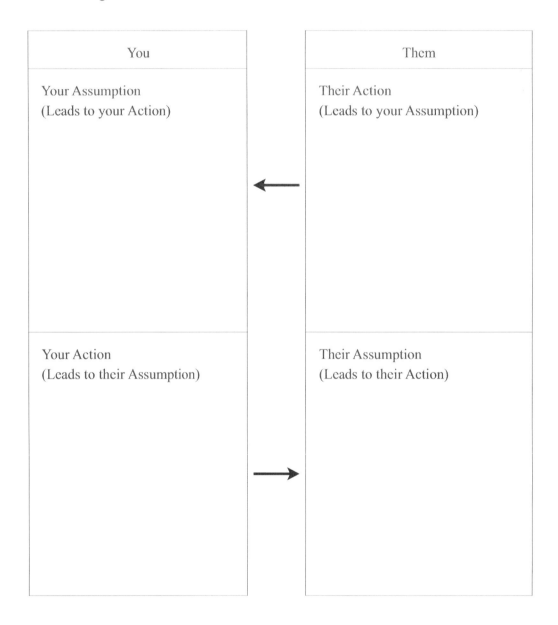

Here's an opportunity for you to change you assumption, which will break the negative pattern and focus your attention on building the relationship.

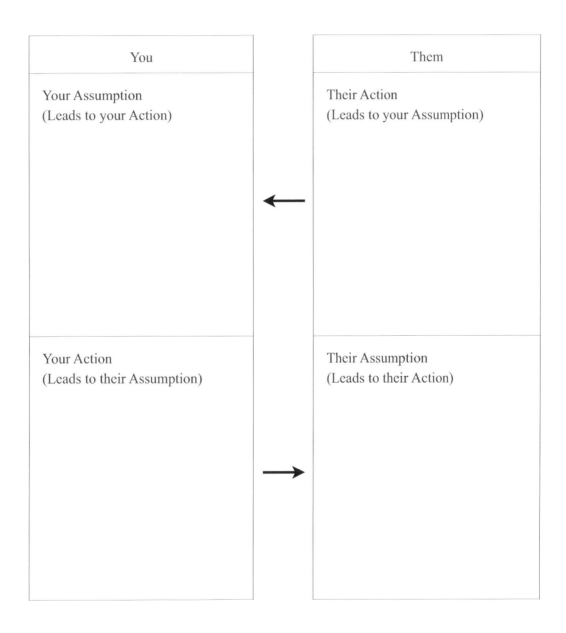

Building Empathy

Excellent communication is essential for a fulfilling life. One of the main ingredients of outstanding communication is empathy. Empathy is the ability to accurately know what another person is feeling and thinking as well as being able to see situations from their point-of-view.

First Level Communication is Listening and Speaking for the Sake of Yourself

Second Level Communication is Listening and Speaking for the Sake of Another and Imagining their experience *From their Point-of-View*

Both Levels of Communication are necessary and valuable. The First Level is not necessarily better or worse than the Second, however, most people spend most of their time in he First Level of Communication. The worksheet below helps you practice Second Level Communication and helps you to further develop an important Emotional Intelligence skill: Empathy.

Person's Name:

From their point-of-view, what is their reality like:

What is most important to them?

What are their biggest dreams?

What are their biggest worries and concerns?

From their Point-of-View :

Person's Name:

From their point-of-view, what is their reality like:

What is most important to them?

What are their biggest dreams?

What are their biggest worries and concerns?

From their Point-of-View :

Session Eight (Personal Leadership, Part 2)

Identifying Your Passions, What You're "Up To" in this world
Leadership Styles based on Core Motivation

Date:

Your Notes:

Your Agreed Action Steps:

Debrief (to be filled out during the week or at the beginning of next session)

What worked?

What didn't work?

What did you learn?

Notes:

Identifying Your Passions

Knowing your passion and nurturing it is a big part of stepping up as a leader. As obvious as it sounds, you have to know what you love and why you love it. With so many career options available, your success at becoming an effective and fulfilled adult relies on your knowing yourself and how you best fit with the world. The starting point is knowing your own passion, and in this session you are invited to explore what you love. The next step is to follow it, design a way that you can act now to nurture your passion and see its impact on your community.

What do you love to do?

If you had two weeks completely free, what would you pursue?

Is there anything odd that you're interested in that most of your friends aren't?

What would you love to pursue as a career?

Leadership Styles with Core Motivation (review of growth and progress)

You've come a long way, and now it's time to look again at your core motivation and the specific challenges and natural styles of leadership.

Leadership is about how well you can work with others and share your vision of what you want to create

Challenges to Effective Leadership	Natural Leadership Styles
Type 1: The Perfectionist Mistakes, errors. Pressure of having so many things to get right. Not being able to stop thinking if what I am doing is good enough. Others blaming me.	When they allow themselves to have fun. When they accept themselves and the situation as perfect just as it is.
Type 2: The Helper Others not recognizing me. Having too much to do for others and not having time for myself. Caring so much about relationships.	When they don't depend on the recognition of others. Focus on action that is also beneficial for themselves as well as others.
Type 3: The Doer Others thinking poorly of them. Inefficiency, things getting in the way of accomplishing a goal. Pressure from having to accomplish a goal.	When they allow themselves to focus on fulfillment. When they can set aside a desire to look good for the sake of accomplishing a meaningful goal.
Type 4: The Artist When others do not acknowledge how I'm feeling, or even worse, when they tell me not to feel that way. Feeling inadequate, abandoned.	When they embrace the ordinary and work to make it exceptional. When they focus on principles, not getting sidetracked by emotions.

Type 5: The Thinker Demands on my time and energy. People invading my space. Being proved factually wrong.	When they take action and connect with people. Thoughtful and astute, 5's have the ability to think deeply about problems to create lasting solutions.
Type 6: The Friend Danger or threats. Not trusting other people. People breaking their promises or being unreliable. Problems.	6's are magnetic when they focus on positive goals and view problems as challenges and opportunities. When they act on positive assumptions.
Type 7: The Optimist Thinking that something better is out there for me. Feeling trapped in something boring or painful. Too many options, not enough time or limits on getting what I want.	When 7's use their natural ability to stir things up for a purpose. When they are willing to face negative situations and emotions and stay focused on creating positive outcomes.
Type 8: The Defender People who take advantage of me or others. Weakness in myself and others. Stupidity. Unfairness. When things are moving slowly or nothing important is really happening.	8's usually have a big impact. As natural leaders 8's truly shine when they take other people's needs and feelings into account.
Type 9: The Peacemaker Having people angry at me. Going along with the plans of others, even if I don't agree with them. Not being able to say 'no.' Seeing possible problems but ignoring them.	When they have a clearly defined goal and they are willing to step outside their comfort zone and take steps to accomplish their goal.

Session Nine (Personal Leadership, Part 3)

Leadership Projects
Mission Statements

Date:

Your Notes:

Your Agreed Action Steps:

Debrief (to be filled out during the week or at the beginning of next session)

What worked?

What didn't work?

What did you learn?

Notes:

Leadership Projects

Whereas mission statements are overarching, a leadership project puts that overarching statement to use. Your leadership project is the intersection of your personal mission and what you want to provide your community.

A leadership project can be short, like helping plan a family vacation that includes meaningful time together, or long, like putting together a business or engaging in an internship. Along the way, you're mission statement gives meaning and a frame to your leadership project, and your leadership project gives a tangible product of your mission statement. The two go hand-in-hand.

The first step is to look for what's needed in your community and determine the impact you want to have on the lives of others.

What's needed in your community?

If you're life were thriving, what gift or service would you offer others?

If you were to accomplish your leadership project, what would be the benefit in the lives of others?

The second step is to revisit your mission statement and determine what project - it may be only a few weeks or it may span a few years - addresses that need in your community and aligns with your mission.

A brainstorm of possible projects:

Choose the top two choices and the next steps to make the project real.

Name of project:

Time frame:

Purpose: Why this, why now?

Break down the larger project into smaller segments
1st Well-Formed Outcome:

2nd Well-Formed Outcome:

3rd Well-Formed Outcome:

Possible adjustments to make:

Name of project:

Time frame:

Purpose: Why this, why now?

Break down the larger project into smaller segments
1st Well-Formed Outcome:

2nd Well-Formed Outcome:

3rd Well-Formed Outcome:

Possible adjustments to make:

Mission Statements

Mission statements are short, personal statements of purpose that inspire, clarify, and focus your emotion, thought, and action. Mission statements are fluid. They grow and change just as you do. They are only as useful as they are used, and the more you use your mission statement and remind yourself of it, the more useful it becomes.

Usually mission statements are short, focus on how you can benefit others, and identify some change you wish to create in your life or in the world.

Date:

Mission statement:

Situations you've used your statement:

Date:

Mission statement:

Situations you've used your statement:

Session Ten (Personal Leadership, Part 4)

Resilience

Celebration

Design the Future

Completion

Date:

Your Notes:

Your Agreed Action Steps:

Debrief (to be filled out during the week or at the beginning of next session)

What worked?

What didn't work?

What did you learn?

Notes:

Resilience

The point of leadership is not being perfect. It's about riding your successes and recovering from your mistakes. The more you learn to recover from setbacks and build up your resiliency the better leader you're going to become. The aim here is to cut down the amount of time it takes for you to recover, and you're at a point when you have many tools to help you do that. This exercise is about finding the perspectives, values, and motivation to build your resilience.

What tools (perspectives, values, future-self, etc.) have worked well for you over the past three months?

What systems have worked well?

Within those systems what has been the key structures you've put in place?

What are examples of when you have recovered quickly? How did you do it? Why do you think it worked so well?

What additional tools can you add to target being resilient?

Celebration

It's important to take time to celebrate the successes. In the fast pace of contemporary life successes quickly become a part of the past while a hunger for yet more in the present and future remains.

In this Wheel, write your current level of satisfaction with each area of your life. Determine your three biggest successes, and celebrate with your coach.

Three biggest successes over the past three months:

Designing the Future

Just like life, after celebration, comes the work of getting to the next level. Incorporating your recent successes - and imagining a new set of success in the coming year - create a vision for yourself a year from now.   From that point in the future, look back on what you have accomplished.

Capture that vision either in a sound recording or draw it out on paper. Then listen to your recording or post the paper in a place you'll often see it. The more you tap into that vision and take action steps while looking at the system you need to use to get there, the more effective and fulfilled your life will become.

Here's space for you to take notes on that vision:

To make the process even more tangible, let's first break down the vision into three Well-Formed Outcomes then look at what systems you can create that will help you achieve that vision.

Well-Formed Outcome #1:

Structures/Systems You Can Add:

Well-Formed Outcome #2:

Structures/Systems You Can Add:

Well-Formed Outcome #3:

Structures/Systems You Can Add:

Completion

Congratulations on finishing the
Academic Life Coaching Program!

Throughout this program you have amassed an impressive set of tools to help you succeed academically, personally, and as a leader.

The program is cyclical. By going back through the exercises, seeing where you were when you went through the first or second time and how far you've come, you bring a new understanding of how you can fit all the parts of the program together. The power of the program isn't in its one time application. These concepts are meant to be woven into your life so that you naturally live your life while being conscious of your values and the choices that you are making. You know how to choose a powerful perspective and recover to it when something knocks you off. You understand the importance of living a life on mission and how exciting it is to start to see a leadership project become a reality.

I invite you to continue your journey and to contribute to the Academic Life Coaching community online through our website and blog, www.academiclifecoaching.com. The more people in this community moving forward, the stronger the tide, and the more everyone benefits.

Now is the time to take a few moments to say what you need to say to be complete with the program and with your coach. And it's a good time to perhaps design how you'll work together in the future.

Made in the USA
Charleston, SC
04 March 2013